JOHANN SEBASTIAN BACH

ORGAN WORKS

BOOK I

EIGHT SHORT PRELUDES AND FUGUES

Edited by

John Dykes Bower & Walter Emery

Order No: NOV 010018

NOVELLO PUBLISHING LIMITED

BOOK I
PREFACE

THREE manuscripts of the Eight Short Preludes and Fugues have been recorded, none of them in Bach's hand. Only two are now in existence. One of these is complete; the other contains only the D minor Prelude and Fugue.

Our edition is based primarily on microfilms of the two extant MSS, but also to some extent on the Peters edition of 1852, whose editor had access to the lost MS.

Players have a right to know, and ought to find out, how far our edition agrees with these sources. All registration, dynamic, pedalling, and metronome marks are editorial, and the ornament interpretations (given in footnotes) are mere suggestions. Our actual corrections are usually indicated by dotted ties, square brackets [ ], superimposed accidentals, and small notes.

As a rule, the reasons for these corrections are obvious;

but some of them require more explanation than can be given in a practical edition such as this. Further, it has been necessary to make a few alterations that cannot be shown in the music text without confusion. Details of these matters will be found in the booklet *Notes on Bach's Organ Works, Book I*, published as a companion to this edition.

The booklet also contains analytical and historical notes, and a discussion of the authenticity of these pieces. There is good reason to believe that they are spurious, and certainly it would be rash to quote them as evidence of Bach's habits in any discussion of his style.

The BWV numbers refer to Schmieder's Thematic Index (Breitkopf, 1950).

J.D.B.
W.E.

May, 1952

The design on the cover is Bach's seal which incorporates his initials

EIGHT SHORT PRELUDES AND FUGUES

I

BWV 553

II

6

III

IV

V

16

18

1) tr

24

2) tr

30

1) 2) Or begin on f♯
Oder beginne bei fis[1]

VI

VII

VIII

Copyright 1952, by Novello & Company, Limited

1) 2)

J S BACH ORGAN WORKS

BOOKS 1, 4 & 5 - *EDITED BY JOHN DYKES BOWER AND WALTER EMERY*
BOOKS 2, 3, 6 TO 12 - *EDITED BY SIR FREDERICK BRIDGE AND JAMES HIGGS*
BOOKS 15 TO 20 - *EDITED BY SIR IVOR ATKINS AND OTHERS*

(The BWV numbers are given in brackets)

BOOK 1: EIGHT SHORT PRELUDES AND FUGUES (553-560)

BOOK 2: MISCELLANEOUS
Allabreve in D major (589)
Prelude in G major (568)
Canzona in D minor (588)
'Giant' Fugue in D minor (680)
Fugue in G minor (131a)
'Little' Prelude and Fugue in E minor (533)
Prelude and Fugue in C minor (549)
Trio in D minor (583)

BOOK 3: MISCELLANEOUS
Five-part Fantasia in C minor (562)
Fugue in B Minor on a subject by Corelli (579)
Prelude and Fugue in A major (536)
'Short' Prelude and Fugue in C major (545)
Fantasia and Fugue in C minor (537)
'Little' Fugue in G minor (578)

BOOK 4: SONATAS FOR TWO MANUALS AND PEDALS
Nos I-III (525-527)

BOOK 5: SONATAS FOR TWO MANUALS AND PEDALS
Nos IV-VI (528-530)

BOOK 6: MISCELLANEOUS
Toccata and Fugue in D minor (565)
Prelude and Fugue in D major (532)
Prelude and Fugue in F minor (534)
Prelude and 'St Anne' Fugue in E flat (552)

BOOK 7: MISCELLANEOUS
'Great' Prelude and Fugue in A minor (543)
'Great' Prelude and Fugue in B minor (544)
'Great' Prelude and Fugue in C minor (546)
Prelude and Fugue in C major (531)
Prelude and Fugue in G major (550)

BOOK 8: MISCELLANEOUS
Toccata in C (or E) (566)
Prelude and 'Wedge' Fugue in E minor (548)
'Great' Prelude and Fugue in G major (541)
Prelude and Fugue in G minor (535)
Fantasia and Fugue in G minor (the 'Great' G minor) (542)

BOOK 9: MISCELLANEOUS
Toccata in C major (564)
Prelude and 'Fiddle' Fugue in D minor (539)
'Great' Prelude and Fugue in C major (547)
Fantasia in G major (572)
Toccata and Fugue in F major (540)

BOOK 10: MISCELLANEOUS
'Dorian' Toccata and Fugue in D minor (538)
Prelude and Fugue in A minor (551)
Passacaglia and Fugue in C minor (582)
Fugue in C minor on a subject by Legrenzi (574)
Prelude in A minor (569)

BOOK 11: FOUR CONCERTOS
(Arrangements of Violin Concertos by Antonio Vivaldi)
Concerto No 1 in G major (592)
Concerto No 2 in A minor (593)
Concerto No 3 in C major (594)
Concerto No 4 (in C major (595)

BOOK 12: MISCELLANEOUS
'Jig' Fugue in G major (577)
Fantasia and Fugue in A minor (561)
Fantasia, with imitation, in B minor (563)
Fantasia in G major (571)
Fugue in D major (580)
Fugue in G major (576)
Prelude in C major (567)
Fantasia in C major (570)
Prelude in C major (943)
Fugue in C minor (575)
Fugue in C major (946)
Pastorale (590)
Trio in C minor (585)
Aria in F (587)

BOOKS 13 & 14:
Now discontinued, these books contained selected Chorale Preludes which are in Books XV to XIX.

BOOK 15: ORGELBÜCHLEIN (The Little Organ Book)

BOOK 16: THE SIX 'SCHÜBLER' CHORALE PRELUDES AND PART III OF THE CLAVIERÜBUNG

BOOK 17: THE 'EIGHTEEN' CHORALE PRELUDES

BOOK 18: MISCELLANEOUS CHORALE PRELUDES (PART I)

BOOK 19: MISCELLANEOUS CHORALE PRELUDES (PART II) AND VARIATIONS

BOOK 20: FOUR-PART HARMONIZATIONS OF THE CHORALES USED IN THE ORGAN WORKS